C000179981

THE CRINAN CANAL

Puffers and Paddle Steamers

by Guthrie Hutton

East meets west at Lochgilphead where the Leith registered coaster 'O' sits at the wharf by Oakfield Bridge. She belonged to the Leith, Hull and Hamburg Steam Packet Company who named their coasters with a single letter of the alphabet and as if that wasn't distinctive enough, they all had very tall funnels. The picture is unusual too, because on this very seasonal canal, photographs taken outside high summer are rare.

© Copyright 1994 Guthrie Hutton
First Published in the United kingdom, 1994
By Richard Stenlake Publishing, Ochiltree Sawmill, The Lade, Ochiltree, Ayrshire KA18 2NX
Telephone: 0290 700266   01290 700266 (from April 1995)
ISBN 1-872074-37-5

In those halcyon Edwardian summer days, before the First World War, a private cruiser eases her way into the sea lock at Crinan. In the background, the little canal steamer Linnet sits in the upper reach.

INTRODUCTION

Sailing round the long barrier of Knapdale and the Mull of Kintyre was dangerous and time consuming in the late eighteenth century and so cutting a canal through it at either Tarbert or Loch Gilp seemed like a good idea. It was first mooted in 1771 when James Watt surveyed the two routes, but it was not until 1792 when canal mania throughout Britain was in full swing, that the Duke of Argyll headed a Company to promote the canal. Loch Gilp was the preferred option and John Rennie surveyed two routes, one to the north of Loch Crinan and another to the south. When Parliament sanctioned the canal in 1793 the final route had not been chosen, although the northern line with a sea lock and harbour at Duntrune was favoured. However, when work began a year and a half later, Rennie had changed his mind.

The cutting started in September 1794 and was expected to take five years, but by 1799 the company was in financial difficulties and having labour troubles too. The Treasury loaned £25,000 and the Commander in Chief of the Army in Scotland loaned some soldiers, but the Company still struggled. It was impossible for them to attract experienced contractors or navvies away from other canal sites to such a remote place and they had to pay high prices for the ones they did get. Some navvies, fearful that the company might not be able to pay them, left the job, while those that remained could name their own price. It was a bad situation and they built a bad canal.

It was opened in 1801, unfinished and with a reduced water level, but while the Company were trying to raise another £25,000 loan to finish it, it was breached and had to be closed. It re-opened eighteen months later in 1806 but was not completed until 1809. A reservoir collapsed and closed it again in 1811 and another Government loan was sought, but by this time the Company and Treasury were both worried. The great Thomas Telford, who was then engineer on the Caledonian Canal, was asked to inspect the Crinan. He could have recommended closure, but instead, suggested a number of improvements that, when implemented in 1817, saved the canal. The Company however was not so fortunate, because when the canal re-opened it was under the management of the Commissioners of the Caledonian Canal. It had, in effect, been nationalised.

Traffic immediately picked up and increased again when the Caledonian Canal was opened in 1822. Steamers could now travel through the two canals from Glasgow to Inverness, but ships were getting bigger and more powerful and by the late 1830's some were also making the trip round the Mull with ease. The only way for the canal to compete, was for a small canal boat to link up with large steamers at each end and in 1839 a service began that was continued by the Linnet up to 1929.

But people still believed in a canal across Kintyre and proposals were put forward in 1846 and again in 1883 for a canal at Tarbert. Similar proposals, to upgrade the Crinan to a single lock ship canal, were made between the 1850's and the First World War, but rejected as unlikely to justify the expense.

So the old canal remained and by 1919, when it became the responsibility of the Ministry of Transport, it was alive with fishing boats and puffers; these busily carving out a place for themselves in Scottish folk lore. In a major reconstruction in the early 1930's, locks and bridges were upgraded and approaches deepened. British Waterways took over in 1962 when commercial use was in decline, but now, with its leaks repaired and tourist potential recognised, the canal is enjoying a new lease of life as a yacht haven; opening another chapter in the enduring story of the Crinan Canal.

Guthrie Hutton, April 1994

In 1851 David Hutcheson and Company took over the steamer services to Ardrishaig and Crinan, and the passenger services on the canal itself. After the Hutchesons had retired, their former partner, David MacBrayne, formed a new company in 1879 to take over the business. There was fierce competition for the tourist traffic from the Clyde to Oban, Fort William and the north. Initially the canal provided the best route, but a new rival steamer operating to Inveraray and the proposal to build a railway line to Oban posed a real threat to the canal route. Hutcheson's responded by building the magnificent Columba. She was made of steel, a new and relatively untried material, but when introduced on the Ardrishaig service in July 1878 became an instant hit. She was the largest steamer on the Clyde at just over 300 feet long and, as this picture shows, extended well beyond the end of the pier, dwarfing the fishing boats beside her.

Arrival of the S. S. "Iona" at Ardrishaig

The route from the Clyde through the Crinan Canal to Fort William and Inverness was called 'The Royal Route', because Queen Victoria and Prince Albert had travelled this way in 1847. It was a brilliantly successful marketing ploy and the route became so popular that Iona, the ship displaced by Columba, was put on a new route to and from Ardrishaig. She left early in the morning for Tarbert, the Kyles of Bute and Wemyss Bay returning, as here, a few minutes after Columba's arrival from Glasgow. Columba always operated the peak day-time service and her appearance at 12.40 was the cue for frantic activity as passengers poured onto the pier to be dispersed to various destinations in Mid-Argyll, or through the canal to the north. At the same time people jostled to board the famous steamer for her return journey to the Clyde; by one o'clock she was under way again and Ardrishaig could return to normal.

The Pier Head and Coaches at Ardrishaig.

Ardrishaig is a canal town. Without the canal there would probably have been no town, no breakwater and no pier (and perhaps no Columba!) So the pier operations were run from the canal office, the large building on the left, which is still used as the canal office by British Waterways. Licences were issued to porters, who wore a large metal badge to indicate their official status, but that didn't stop small boys from trying to get a slice of the action too. Pier dues were included in the price of a ticket for those passengers continuing their journey by canal, but others, including local people who just wanted to go onto the pier, had to pay. Coaches waited in the square to take passengers on to other destinations, but when motor transport replaced the horses and tarmac roads replaced dirt tracks, it was buses, operated by MacBrayne's themselves, that brought an end to canal passenger services.

6

The breakwater was originally built to protect the canal entrance, but as the harbour developed and steamers got bigger the breakwater was progressively extended to protect them. The approach to the sea lock also had to be continually improved, initially because it was too shallow and hampered by dangerous rocks, but latterly as part of the improvements done in the early 1930's. The sea lock was re-built at this time, beside the original, but closer to the breakwater and further out to sea. The swing bridge carrying the main road to Kintyre, which had spanned the old lock chamber, was also replaced, by a new bridge across the head of the new lock. The picture shows the canal dredger working in front of the sea lock, possibly as part of the re-building operations. Prominent in the background is the Parish Church, built in 1860.

ANCE TO CRINAN CANAL, ARDRISHAIG.

The puffer Glenrosa was a regular on the canal after the Second World War. She seems enormous here, nosing, empty, into the sea lock at Ardrishaig. She started life as a wartime 'victualling inshore craft' with a number, VIC 29, instead of a name. The Ministry of War Transport built 54 of these steam, and 9 diesel, puffers during the Second World War to carry stores to larger ships. The design was based on two puffers, the Anzac and the Lascar, which had been built by Scott & Sons at Bowling in 1939. Most were built in England and worked at English ports, although some were even shipped to work at overseas bases. Glenrosa was on the Thames when she was bought after the war by G&G Hamilton of Brodick and brought north, one of more than a dozen VIC's bought by Clyde owners. She was wrecked off the Island of Mull some years later.

ENTRANCE TO CRINAN CANAL, ARDRISHAIG.

A.2738.

The small basin at Ardrishaig is usually crowded with boats of all kinds either resting after reaching the haven of the canal or before leaving it for the often turbulent waters of the Clyde. But when this private launch passed between the sea lock and Lock 2 in 1935 there appeared to be only one other boat in the basin, the puffer Petrel. She was launched in 1897 at Larne for her first owner, James Burrows. Her next owners, Warnock of Paisley sold her to McNeil's of Greenock who used her for sand dredging off Cardross. There she met a violent end on 19th April 1951, when her boiler exploded. The old sea lock can be seen between the Petrel's stern and the cruiser's bow. It was used for a time as a dry dock after being replaced, but today simply forms part of the basin.

Boats have to turn sharply in the basin because the sea lock and Lock 2 enter it at 90° to each other. Lock size was important to the canal promoters, too large and a lot of water would be lost with each locking operation, too small and the canal would not attract enough customers. Rennie intended to build all of the eastern locks, like Lock 2 here, with dressed stone from Arran. To do that, the locks at Ardrishaig had to be finished first and then the canal flooded to take the stone to Cairnbaan by water. But the locks at Ardrishaig were delayed and the Cairnbaan locks had to be built with local rubble. Mr.Rennie was not pleased! Behind Lock 2, in this picture from the 1870's, fishing nets are drying on wooden frames known as 'the stances'; one of the most distinctive sights in Ardrishaig when the herring fishery was at its height.

Locks 2 and 3 are separated by a short, boomerang shaped, pound. Above it was the canal manager's house, a large and imposing Victorian villa that has recently been converted into a hotel. The high sided pound was unsuitable for moorings, so boats preferred to lie in the lower basin, while most of the town's canal related activity happened on the pound between Lock 3 and Lock 4. Here, the puffer Hafton, is approaching Lock 3 from the west, in a picture from 1924. She was very much a canal puffer, built in 1910 at the McNicoll brothers Kelvin Dock yard at Maryhill on the Forth and Clyde Canal. The yard had a reputation for building good, sound boats, but puffers were often worked to the limit of their capabilities and Hafton was lost in the Firth of Lorne in 1933. The private cruiser on the right is alongside the berth used for a time by the passenger steamer Linnet.

Ardrishaig and Lochgilphead

The Linnet is seen here in the 1880's heading for Lock 4, past Munro's boatyard (the yard can also be seen to the left of Hafton on the previous page, with a maintenance barge alongside). Beyond the canal, the main town of Ardrishaig is seen sandwiched between the canal and Loch Gilp, with Lochgilphead in the distance. Boatbuilding was one of Ardrishaig's principal industries and although Archibald and Donald Munro's yard was on the canal, their reputation was for building good sea boats, mainly for the fishing industry. Fleets from Ullapool to Campbelltown had Ardrishaig built boats in them. Boat building reached its peak at the same time as the herring fishery in the 1880's. The Loch Fyne boats were open decked and required great handling skills, particularly if the crew decided to try their luck in less sheltered waters.

H. M. S. "Daisy", Crinan Canal, Ardrishaig.

Before the turn of the century, the important Loch Fyne herring fishery was policed by a fisheries protection cruiser, HMS Jackal, based at Ardrishaig. She drew unwelcome attention to herself when she fired warning shots at a boat fishing with a prohibited trawl net on the east shore of Loch Fyne at Otter Ferry. A fisherman was killed, but the inquest exonerated the sailors who 'had only been doing their duty'. Jackal was later replaced by the cutter, HMS Daisy. She was much smaller, with a crew of only six and can be seen here below Lock 4, beside Munro's boatyard. Behind her is the Ark, an appropriately named floating hut which was used as temporary accommodation for canal employees. She was sunk when ice was pushed into her side by a passing vessel, but was raised and is still on the canal near Crinan Bridge. Daisy was wrecked in 1913 and not replaced.

Main Street, Ardrishaig

CHALMERS STREET FROM SOUTH, ARDRISHAIG, LOCH FYNE.   B.8772.

Although these two pictures from 1888 and 1953 are separated by sixty five years, they show that little changed in that time. But Ardrishaig's main street is unrecognisable now. The buildings on the left were replaced in 1960 by a characterless block and in an attempt to emulate Lochgilphead's open front to the sea, all the buildings on the right were demolished in the 1970's. At the beginning of the nineteenth century, when people started to arrive in the new town there were few buildings for them to stay in and some had to live in tents. Many of the early inhabitants came from Ayrshire, attracted by the fishing industry. Most of the town's industry was related to either the canal, the fishing or both, but you were in a separate social class if you had a canal job, because that was steady. In Ardrishaig you were either rich, poor, or worked on the canal.

This bridge across the chamber of Lock 4 is the only other road crossing of the canal in Ardrishaig. It gives access to the road that runs along the west bank of the canal to Oakfield Bridge at Lochgilphead. Local people had distrusted the safety of bridges for a long time before this bridge was installed at the end of the nineteenth century, as part of a general upgrading of all canal bridges by the then engineer in charge, William Rhodes. The present bridge replaced it in the 1930's. Rhodes was appointed in 1868-9 after a succession of incompetent or corrupt engineers. The canal engineer was a very powerful figure in Ardrishaig and, miles away from official scrutiny, could do more or less what he pleased, but Rhodes took his responsibilities seriously and he and his successor L. John Groves made significant improvements to the canal.

S.S. „Linnet" on Crinan Canal   Ardrishaig

The Linnet was built for David Hutcheson and Co. to replace the horse drawn passenger boats in 1866. This quaint little boat with her tall red funnel must have seemed heaven sent to photographers on the tourist trail and she is, by far, the most commonly photographed subject on the Scottish Canals. At Ardrishaig, pictures show her at two different terminals. In this one from around 1900, she is seen approaching a berth above Lock 3. Her horse drawn predecessors used to stop above Lock 4 but Linnet must have come down to Lock 3 to reduce the walk for passengers from the pier. Not that they had to carry their luggage, that was taken separately to Crinan (by road!) because there was no room on the Linnet. On the extreme right, the sign advises people that this is where they should join the steamer Linnet 'for Oban and the North'.

S.S. LINNET, CRINAN CANAL. 1436. J.V.

The Linnet operated for only four months every year and the ritual of putting up her signs was the signal to Ardrishaig folk that summer and 'the season' had arrived. The signpost on the right of this picture from 1878 is interesting because it directs passengers 'to the steamer Iona for Glasgow and the South' and must therefore pre-date the Columba's maiden voyage by only a few weeks, unless of course somebody forgot to change the sign. The Linnet is lying at the old boat terminal above Lock 4 and, towards the end of her career, she is seen using it all the time, suggesting that she changed terminals more than once. In the background of the picture is the Royal Hotel, which apparently changed its name from the Poltalloch Posting House after Queen Victoria walked through a floral arch beside it, on her way up the path to join her specially decorated boat on the canal.

The Crinan is a maritime short cut rather than an inland waterway and so craft that spent their working lives on it are rare. Most, like the Linnet, served the needs of coastal shipping. The early steamers could go through the canal, but later, track boats, boats that could be 'tracked' or towed by horses, were put on to link up at each end with larger steamers. The first boat, Thornwood, started to operate in 1839 and was later either renamed Maid of Perth or replaced by another boat of that name, but it was Sunbeam, the sleek boat on the left of this picture, that became famous when she took Queen Victoria through the canal. There were pipers at every lock, but despite their efforts and those of the horses and their scarlet clad postilions, the Queen found the delays in the locks tiresome. Not perhaps the best start for 'The Royal Route'. Across the canal from Sunbeam is the 20 ton sailing coaster, Hope.

One of the major canalside industries in Ardrishaig was the Glenfyne Distillery. It was on the west bank at Kilduskland, beyond the trees in the background of this picture of 1920's yachts. It started to operate in 1831 and kept going until 1937, but it has now been demolished. The chapel at Kilduskland disappeared long ago, but its presence is still felt. People tell of hearing monastic music and of seeing ghostly monks on the canal bank or standing where the monastery gardens once were, or even rising out of the canal! But if anyone had an excuse to do a bit of haunting it was the young robber who lived at the head of the Kilduskland Glen. He was forced to live wild because of the part he had played in a local clan feud, but his enemies finally trapped him at his den on the edge of a cliff and set fire to it. His only escape was to jump; onto their upturned spears below.

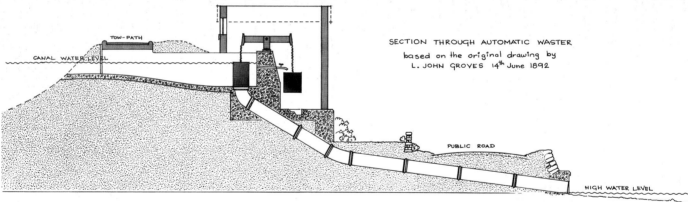

SECTION THROUGH AUTOMATIC WASTER
based on the original drawing by
L. JOHN GROVES 14th June 1892

TOW-PATH

CANAL WATER LEVEL

PUBLIC ROAD

HIGH WATER LEVEL

Water control has always been a problem in this wet and mountainous country, and on the western edge of Ardrishaig is an ingenious solution to the problem; the 'automatic waster', built in 1895 to regulate the level of the pound between Ardrishaig and Cairnbaan. A large bucket at one end of a chain sits like a plug in the outlet sluice. The chain passes over a rocker arm to another bucket which fills with water when the canal rises above its designed level. When the second bucket outweighs the first it tips the mechanism and releases a roaring cascade down an outlet pipe to the sea, 32 feet below. This remarkable piece of canal engineering sits in a very unremarkable stone shed beside the towpath, but British Waterways have considerately fitted a window and installed a plaque to let towpath users see what's inside. The picture above, from1878, is located to the west of where the autowaster was built.

Children used to run alongside the Linnet on the long reach from Ardrishaig past Lochgilphead to Cairnbaan throwing flowers to the passengers. This local tradition stemmed from Queen Victoria's visit, but the real purpose of following the boat was the hope that passengers would throw money to them. Any coin that fell between two would prompt a mad scramble for possession. An edict issued in 1887 sought to discourage these practices, but this picture from 1905 shows youngsters still following the Linnet, in hope. The picture also shows how well the Linnet's canoe shaped hull slid though the water causing minimal wash. She could travel at speed without endangering the canal banks, unlike the early paddle steamers, who raced each other along the canal causing considerable damage.

The S. S. "Conway" at Lochgilphead, Crinan Canal.

The Linnet could only take 270 passengers, substantially less than the Columba, and at the height of the season, during the Glasgow Fair and other Clydeside trades holidays, a relief boat was needed. To begin with the Sunbeam was used, but later the canal ice breaker Conway (not needed for breaking ice, even in a Scottish summer) was chartered to take the extra passengers. It is likely that some also went by road. Here the Conway is seen approaching Oakfield Bridge beside Lochgilphead; a distant Linnet can be seen ahead of her, partly obscured by the gate on the extreme right of the picture. In winter, Conway's bow was designed to ride up on top of the ice, which was smashed by the weight of the boat. The wharf beside the bridge was built as one of the improvements recommended by Thomas Telford in 1817. An early puffer, with a tall funnel and no shelter for the helmsman, sits alongside it.

Crinan Canal, Lochgilphead.

The puffer lazing at the wharf on this long hot summer's day is the Cretan, another Forth and Clyde Canal boat, built at Kirkintilloch in 1910 for J and J Hay Ltd. The wharf was the main discharge point for Lochgilphead and was used by a host of puffers and also by MacBrayne's two small steamers Handa and Brenda as MacBrayne's had a depot near the bridge. The bridge keeper at the end of last century was a William Miller, who also doubled as the local coal merchant, with a yard beside the bridge. He became so closely identified with the bridge that people called it Miller's Bridge and they still call it Miller's Bridge today - although the official name is Oakfield Bridge. The canal was built with towpaths on each side, which have survived most completely between the bridge and Ardrishaig. West of the bridge the path on the south side is now less distinct.

LOCHGILPHEAD

210422

The Canal Company had to pay two and a half times their estimate for land at Oakfield to one of their own proprietors, John McNeill of Gigha. He was clearly not going to let this golden opportunity slip because he also set about planning the development of Ardrishaig and Lochgilphead on his land. Lochgilphead is the more obviously planned town. Poltalloch Street and Lochnell Street form the sea front and the main street, Argyll Street, meets them at right angles at Colchester Square. The fine Georgian buildings on the west side of the square date from the 1820's, while this east side was built by a local architect and builder, David Crow, in 1841. Markets and fairs were held on the green, the reclaimed land at the head of Loch Gilp, in the foreground of this picture. The war memorial was designed by Dr. Colin Sinclair, a Glasgow architect from a Lochgilphead family.

24

ARGYLL STREET. LOCHGILPHEAD.

Dr. Sinclair also designed the Stag Hotel, the conical roofed building on the left of this picture of Argyll Street. At the top of the street, the Parish Church was built in 1885 by another Glasgow architect, John Honeyman. It replaced a church built in 1828 to a standard design by Thomas Telford, one of a number throughout the Highlands. The main industries of the town were mills, set along the south bank of the swiftly flowing Cuilarstich Burn, a distillery, a ropeworks, and of course, fishing. The population had reached 1000 in 1825, rose to 1700 in 1851, fell to just over 900 as some of those industries declined and has recovered to around 1000 today. Lochgilphead became the headquarters of the Argyllshire Constabulary in 1840 and replaced Inveraray and Dunoon as the administrative centre for Argyll in 1890. It is still the headquarters of Argyll and Bute District Council.

The good news for the engineers in Oakfield Moss was that the cutting got down to a bed of clay which they could use to line the peaty banks, the bad news was that they also encountered rock, which the Highland navvies left for another day, preferring to dig the soft peat instead. Cutting canals across boggy ground was always difficult and the Crinan was no exception. The embankment across Oakfield Moss sank nine feet during construction and in January 1805 a flood destroyed 70 yards of it, closing the canal for over a year. A new line for the canal was cut on the firmer, high ground to the south. The original embankment can still be seen amongst the trees, inside the more exaggerated bend of the new canal, in this picture of the Linnet heading east from Cairnbaan - still with her attendant young hopefuls on the towpath.

"S.S. LINNET" AT CAIRNBAAN HOTEL, CRINAN CANAL

Cairnbaan takes its name from a bronze age burial mound on the south side of the canal called, in Gaelic, Carn Ban (white cairn). Here 4 miles of lock free canal comes to an end and Lock 5 is the start of a climb through four locks and three short pounds to the summit of the canal. A swing bridge, installed in the 1930's, spans the head of Lock 5. It replaced the earlier bridge which crossed the lock chamber itself. At Cairnbaan the double towpaths are now used as roads, the one on the south side incorporated into the main route to Knapdale and Loch Sween. Here the Linnet is slightly obscured by a maintenance barge as she leaves Lock 5 for Ardrishaig. In the background is the Cairnbaan Hotel which was built as an inn at the same time as the canal and has catered for canal travellers ever since. British Waterways have recently established a winter boat park beside Lock 5.

Meeting a large, ungainly, puffer in the narrow confines of the canal could be an un-nerving experience for a small cabin cruiser. Here somebody's pride and joy gives Colin MacNeill's Stronshira a wide berth as she emerges from Lock 6. The tranquility of this summer scene makes it hard to imagine the terrifying force of the water that burst out of the Glen Clachaig reservoir in January 1811. It smashed the lower gates of Lock 6 and washed away part of the road between Locks 5 and 6. Glen Clachaig was one of a number of reservoirs built in the Knapdale Hills to supply the canal with water. In February 1859, Cam Loch, the highest reservoir in the system, burst. Water swept through the lower reservoirs and on down the hill to fill the summit of the canal with rubble and mud. Winters in these parts can be wild, wet and unpredictable.

For over sixty years however there was one very predictable thing about Cairnbaan summers. The appearance of the Linnet; and with her, the photographers. Their pictures show her between locks, in locks and as these two shots at Lock 7 show, going in and out of locks. The Linnet had priority over all other vessels and the operation of the canal was geared to her timetable. It took under two hours for her to go from one end to the other and locks and bridges were set to allow an unimpeded passage. She was a twin screw vessel and her two, two cylinder, engines exhausted up the funnel, to produce the necessary draught for the fires. It also produced a lot of smoke and the funnel was specially tall to throw it away from passengers on the decks. When she first appeared she had no bridge (see page 17) but this was added later and the machinery was controlled from it.

The "ALBEMARLE" Series. Stereoscopic Slides. Copyright.

The "ALBEMARLE" Series. Stereoscopic Slides. Copyright.

6061   on the Crinan Canal

The canal's early promoters expected it to provide a great stimulus to fishing on the west coast, and so it did, allowing easier access to fishing grounds and to the growing market in Glasgow. Ardrishaig became a main centre for the Loch Fyne herring fleet, Crinan thrived as a fishing port and the canal buzzed with boats changing grounds. In later years fishermen from Tarbert drove cars across the Kintyre peninsular to assess the fishing on the west side, before committing themselves to a canal passage. Now the reduced fleets are confined to distant harbours and few boats use the canal. This 'turn of the century' stereoscopic picture shows a small boat going through Lock 7. Stereoscopes were popular in Victorian and Edwardian times; the two slightly different pictures, viewed through a special device, appeared three dimensional. But please don't cut up the book to try it!

S. S. "Linnet" Loch 8,   Crinan Canal.

The Linnet's twice daily arrival at the eastern summit lock, Lock 8, would have been greeted with great anticipation by the little Cairnbaan Stores and Post Office. The Linnet was like a crowded wee bus and was the only passenger boat in MacBrayne's fleet to have no restaurant. Refreshments ashore were therefore eagerly sought by passengers and so too were souvenirs and picture post-cards, some of which will have found their way into this book. People were only too happy to get off and stretch their legs and once on dry land, they could walk between the locks and even stroll along the summit reach, safe in the knowledge that the boat had to stop at the next locks. The canal is only nine miles long and with nine locks to delay the boat, passengers who wanted to save money, in the days of the old track boats, walked the whole way.

THE CAMP, CAIRNBAAN.

A.5445

This Ministry of Labour work camp was built before the Second World War and it may also have been used by the Forestry Commission when they started planting at Knapdale in the 1930's. The Crinan Canal is famous for running short of water and a new reservoir was needed to compensate for so many thirsty new trees in the catchment area. The forest enhances a previously barren landscape and some beautiful walks have been laid out in it. The Commission has plans for selective thinning and replanting with a mixture of species, including native broadleaved trees, which will further enhance the area. During the War the camp was used as a prisoner of war camp and some Italian prisoners escaped from it (Italians were often used on forestry work). They were recaptured at Tayvallich, although the popular story is that they were turned back by that fearsome local equivalent of barbed wire; midges.

32

These thatched croft houses beside the canal at Daill seem incongruous beside a canal that was at the forefront of engineering technology in its day. It must have been a shocking imposition on such remote communities. Beyond the crofts, on the other side of the canal, is Loch a Bharain. Loch and canal are in effect the same body of water and the towpath is like a causeway with a small bridge which can be seen on the left above the houses. A small burn feeds the loch and the water level is maintained by a sluice mechanism hidden in the trees on the far side. Water control has always been a problem in this wet and hilly country, but the loss of water through leaks, coupled with heavy seasonal use in summer, often resulted in operational restrictions. British Waterways have done substantial work recently to remedy the problem.

CRINAN CANAL FROM ABOVE LOCK 9, CAIRNBAAN.   A.5673.

The summit of the canal is 64 feet above sea level and only 1114 yards long. Here, with the summit behind her, a yacht emerges from Lock 9 heading west. Beside the lock is the old boathouse where the Linnet was kept during the winter and from where she emerged, like a butterfly, in the late spring, resplendent and ready for the new season. The picture from 1937 shows the boathouse still in reasonable condition, eight years after the Linnet had left it for the last time. It soon became a roofless shell and is now a forlorn ruin. The boathouse of her trackboat predecessors, which may have been at the same location, was ruined in the Cam Loch dam burst in 1859 and the two boats had to be dug out of the wreckage to work individually in the coming season, one below Dunardry Locks and the other below Cairnbaan, while the summit was closed.

This puffer in Lock 9 is about to head east along the summit, her crew no doubt grateful they didn't have to "double the Mull" as a trip round the Mull of Kintyre was called. This little song shows the puffermen's preference for the calmer waters of the canal

Oh! the Crinan Canal for me,
I don't like the wild raging sea,
It would be too terrific to cross the Pacific,
Or sail to Japan or Fiji.
A life on the Spanish Main,
I think it would drive me insane,
The big foaming breakers would give me the shakers,
The Crinan Canal for me.

    chorus:
    Oh! the Crinan Canal for me,
    I don't like the wild raging sea,
    The big foaming breakers would give me the shakers,
    The Crinan Canal for me.

It's the Crinan Canal for me,
From sea terrors there you are free,
There's no shark or whale that would make you turn pale,
Or shiver and shake at the knee.
I would nae like leavin' ma bones,
In a locker beside Davy Jones,
From Ardrishaig to Crinan's the best trip A'hve bin in,
The Crinan Canal for me.

    chorus:

Aye the Crinan Canal for me,
It's neither too big nor too wee,.
Oh! it's lovely and calm when you're fryin' your ham,
Or makin' a nice cup of tea.
You can go for a stroll on its banks,
To loosen your muscle bound shanks,
You can darn your socks while you're still in its locks,
The Crinan Canal for me.

    chorus:

DUNARDRY LOCKS, CRINAN CANAL (1)

The puffer Spartan, here heading up out of Lock 10, was built as VIC 18 by J Hay & Sons Ltd. at Kirkintilloch. Hay's built two VIC boats, but the Ministry of War Transport only took delivery of one and the other joined Hay's fleet as the Kaffir. After the war, the Ministry handed VIC 18 to Hay's as compensation for the loss of one of their boats, which had been requisitioned during the war. She was renamed Spartan, the third puffer to bear the name and converted to diesel in 1961. She is still afloat as an exhibit at the Scottish Maritime Museum at Irvine in Ayrshire. Puffers were a development of Forth and Clyde Canal barges and many were built on that canal to fit through its locks, which were a little narrower and 20 feet shorter than the Crinan's. It is ironic that these boats were originally built for another canal than the one they came to be so closely identified with.

There are five locks in the Dunardry flight with small basins between them. Building locks out of rubble was not an exact science and Lock 11, seen here in 1885, settled unevenly on sandy foundations with the walls off true, it leaked and was the tightest fit. So when Ross and Marshall's puffer Sealight was being built in 1930, the designers came to measure the lock and build the boat to fit. What they didn't know was that the cill of Lock 5 projected further into the chamber than the other lock cills and the new puffer had to return ignominiously to Ardrishaig to offload some of her cargo before she could continue her journey. The bridge across the lock chamber here is the original, but Lock 11's foundations also caused problems for the swing bridge that replaced it and it too had to be replaced in 1900 by the canal's only traversing bridge, which is still in operation today.

S.S. "LINNET" AT DUNARDY LOCH, CRINAN CANAL.

Lock keepers and their families were able to indulge in a little bit of free enterprise by selling produce to the passing boats and the Linnet offered rich pickings. Cows were tethered beside tables in front of lock houses, like this one at Lock 13, to provide fresh milk and there was home baking and home made lemonade available too. Clearly some of the sales pitches were a bit heavy because the Canal Office issued a notice in 1887 only permitting such activity 'on the understanding that no annoyance is caused to passengers', who were encouraged to report any such inconvenience to canal officials. Puffers were also a source of 'trade', coal being exchanged for produce from the lock keeper's garden and fishermen too left fish for lock and bridge keepers as they passed. To-day, tourists can picnic at lockside tables made from old lock gates.

ON THE CRINAN CANAL, CAIRNBAAN.

A.5672.

West of Dunardry Locks the character of the landscape changes dramatically with the rugged forested hills of Knapdale on the south side of the canal and the wide, boggy expanse of the Moine Mhor (the great moss) to the north - two archetypal fantasy kingdoms, and between them, the canal. At the northern edge of the Moine Mhor, and just out of view to the left of this picture of a 1930's cruiser, is Dunadd, a hill fort on a prominent rock outcrop, that was once capital of the ancient kingdom of Dalriada. The sea still covered the Moine Mhor when the Scots invaded from Ireland around 500AD to establish their kingdom, but the native Picts continued to dispute ownership of Dunadd for over 300 years and some rock carvings on the fort are Pictish in origin. The Scots finally gained the upper hand when Kenneth Macalpine was crowned king over all Scotland in 843AD.

The canal was considered inadequate for the transportation of livestock and so, before sheep and cattle were moved by lorry, the roads around the canal were often crowded with animals making their own way to Ardrishaig. They would then be shipped to markets on the steamers and Ardrishaig harbour is reckoned to have handled more sheep than people in some years. The town could often find itself taken over by noisy flocks which were sometimes kept overnight at the small park by the monument or nearby at Brackly. No doubt some steamer passengers were surprised to have a flock of sheep for company, while it was no surprise to some local men to have to clean up the town after each invasion. Here a flock of sheep crowd the road at Dunardry while a kilted tourist keeps his excited dog at barking distance down the canal bank.

BELLANOCH BRIDGE, CRINAN CANAL.

2/9466.J.V.

The canal was cut into the hills at Bellanoch because it was impossible to pile firm foundations in the moss. The road north across the Moine Mhor crosses the canal at Bellanoch on a swing bridge that rests on abutments hewn from solid rock. Heading through the bridge in this 1933 picture is the puffer Jennie on her way to Crinan. She was built at Larne in 1902 for Calum Campbell but became stranded in a fog on Eigg in 1954 and was lost. The car sits opposite where the little Bellanoch garage used to be, just out of the picture. It thrived on the cross roads created by the bridge and the road south across Knapdale to Tayvallich and Loch Sween. At Bellanoch too the road north crosses the mouth of the River Add as it flows into lovely Loch Crinan. From here to Crinan the views from the towpath are breathtaking and surely unsurpassed on any canal in Britain.

CRINAN CANAL, CRINAN FERRY AND DUNTROON CASTLE
FROM BELLANOCH

B. 7995

An embankment was built across Bellanoch Bay to create this very un-canal like lagoon, but it was not built well. During construction it slipped and sank into the soft sea mud before it was stabilised, and poor finishing meant that it leaked badly at the western end. Today it is one of the canal's greatest assets, as a haven for the yachts that are now the most prolific users of the canal. Rows of gleaming thoroughbreds lie in the peat black water, in startling contrast to the simple whitewashed austerity of the old Bellanoch kirk, which looks down on them from the hills. In the foreground of this 1960's view is the old schoolhouse. Below it is the school which a local Community Business plans to open as a visitor centre. The canal dredger chugging along the channel shows how large the lagoon is; beyond it is Loch Crinan, Crinan Ferry and Duntrune Castle.

" Duntroon Castle."

If Rennie's original plan for a canal along the north side of Loch Crinan had been pursued, then Duntrune Castle would have made a spectacular backdrop to the proposed harbour. It stands on a rocky promontory that was probably a fortified site long before the six foot thick courtyard wall was built at the end of the thirteenth century. A seventeenth century house now stands within the wall, along with more recent additions, and can be seen projecting above it in this picture. With first Dunadd and then Duntrune guarding it, the entrance to Loch Crinan was clearly of strategic importance in the past and the wealth of archaeological remains in the surrounding area and north to Kilmartin would indicate a sizeable civilisation living here in early times. Duntrune was later a Campbell stronghold and featured in some nasty clan feuds.

The Maggie was a puffer too, in fact she was two puffers, J Hay and Sons Ltd's sister ships, Boer and Inca, which both played the starring role in Alexander (Sandy) Mackendrick's 1954 Ealing comedy film, 'The Maggie'. With a cargo gained under false pretences, the Maggie escapes down the Clyde to the canal where the crew indulge in a spot of poaching. The owner of the cargo catches up with them and his agent gets caught up in the poaching. The poachers are chased by the Laird, his factor and the local constable, the Laird falls in the canal, the factor catches the unfortunate agent and the puffer's crew get clean away; wonderful, and so real! This 'production still' shows the filming on the canal. But perhaps the most famous puffer to be immortalised on screen is the Vital Spark which, with her skipper Para Handy, has featured in a number of television comedy series' produced by BBC Scotland.

CRINAN BRIDGE CRINAN CANAL.

224203.

The ferry that crossed Loch Crinan to Crinan Ferry has long since ceased to operate. Crinan Bridge gave access to it, but is now just used by maintenance vehicles. The bridge is also known as Puddler's Bridge and the cottage beside it, Puddler's Cottage. Puddling is the process whereby clay and sand are mixed with water into a paste which is then liberally applied to the bed and sides of the canal to create a watertight seal. The puddler, whose job was to inspect the canal for leaks and plug them with puddle clay, lived here, hence the name. Presumably his base was at the western end of the canal because the original finishing of this section had been so poor. The puffer heading west through the bridge, in this picture from 1933, is the Briton. She was built at Kirkintilloch in 1896 for J and J Hay.

S.S. "Linnet" at Crinan

Like Loch Gilp, the shallow water of Loch Crinan meant that the canal had to be cut some way along the shore to reach deep water for the sea lock, but at Crinan the excavation was through hard rock. It was slow work and the finished canal was very narrow, with tight bends and a very dangerous jagged edge. A number of boats sank after hitting it and one of Telford's improvements was to erect wooden fenders, nevertheless one boat is said to have sunk every three years between 1885 and 1921 and when the canal closed briefly in 1878, fifteen tons of lost propellers were recovered from a rocky bend. The dangers of the cutting are clear in this picture of Linnet leaving Crinan. Behind her the little arched bridge is over a spillway which, like the automatic waster in the east, is used to control the level of the pound between Dunardry and Crinan, although here the sluices are set manually.

The Linnet's berth above Lock 14 at Crinan was just a short walk away from the steamer pier and although they didn't go as fast as modern passenger transport, the rapid turnaround of these boats could learn nothing from the present day. The steamer at the pier is the Chevalier, which operated the Crinan leg of the Royal Route more than any other steamer. She set off from Corpach at the southern end of the Caledonian Canal in the early morning and called at Fort William and Ballachulish before picking up most of her passengers at Oban for their journey south to Crinan. The Chevalier was a well cared for ship because while the Linnet was charging along the canal to Ardrishaig and back, the crew had time to scrub and polish until she shined in welcome for the new passengers heading north. She returned to the Clyde in the winter, but was damaged in a storm on the Ardrishaig run in March, 1927 and had to be scrapped.

The Royal Route had become somewhat passé by 1929 when the buses ended not only the Linnet's canal services, but the steamer services to Oban and the north too. Before that the railways from Glasgow to Oban and Fort William had taken some of the traffic away, but despite a proposal to build a line from Glasgow in 1887, railways never directly threatened the canal. The Linnet was sold to the Glasgow Motor Boat Racing Club who moored her, as a club house, at Shandon in the Gareloch where she was wrecked in a January storm in 1932. In the background of this pre-First World War picture of the Linnet preparing for another run to the east, is Lock14, which was hewn out of solid rock and topped with rubble and dressed stone from Morven. It was made to the same dimensions as the two sea locks to give access to a dry dock, which the Canal Company then couldn't afford to build.

THE HARBOUR, CRINAN, ARGYLL. B.5278.

The sea locks were made bigger than the inland locks to allow coastal vessels into the canal harbours. Crinan harbour used to be crowded with puffers and fishing boats, but now, in the season, it is filled with yachts. Some are there while cruising the west coast, but others are there for the racing. For many years the Clyde Cruising Club's Tobermory Race was the highlight. It took place at the Glasgow Fair weekend and huge numbers of boats raced to Ardrishaig and then passed through the canal on one hectic day. The race attracts fewer boats now and the focus has shifted to West Highland Week, a series of races, over eight days at the beginning of August. Fleets converge on Loch Crinan from various places and from there set off for Oban in a spectacular mass start. Crinan used to be a remote spot called Port Righ (Port of the King) but the canal changed everything, even the name.

CRINAN FROM WEST.   90697. J.V.

Much of this view, looking east across the sea lock in 1923, had changed a few years later. The sea lock, like the one at Ardrishaig, was replaced in the early 1930's by a new one excavated out of land in the foreground of the picture. It was beside the old lock which remained in place as an extension to the basin. In front of the Linnet, on the reach above Lock 14, is MacBrayne's little cargo boat Brenda. She was designed for the run through the canal to Mull, Fort William and Inverness, but was taken off and broken up in 1929, the same year that the Linnet ceased operations. At least the puffers, two of which seem to guard the entrance to the sea lock, kept going for a few more years. Ships at sea always had a theoretical right of entry to the canal 24 hours a day, depending on the state of tide, which meant that the sea lock keepers had to be on call all night. That's changed too!

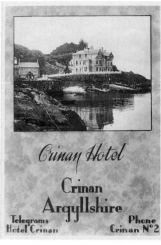

Crinan Hotel

Crinan
Argyllshire

Telegrams
Hotel Crinan

Phone
Crinan N° 2

TARIFF

Bedroom, Single, from	6/-
Bedroom, Double. ,,	12/-
Breakfast,	3/-
Lunch,	3/6
Plain Tea,	1/6
High Tea,	3/-, 3/6
Dinner,	6/-

Terms per week till end of June,
£5 5 0 to £5 15 0

July, August and September
£5 10 0 to £6 10 0

Those Charges are Inclusive.

Apartments with full Board and Baths.

Private Sittingrooms	7/6 per day.
Private Lock-up Garage,	1/6 per day.

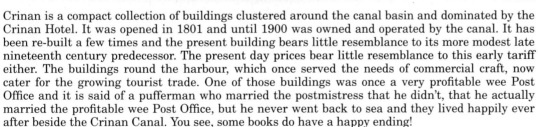

Crinan is a compact collection of buildings clustered around the canal basin and dominated by the Crinan Hotel. It was opened in 1801 and until 1900 was owned and operated by the canal. It has been re-built a few times and the present building bears little resemblance to its more modest late nineteenth century predecessor. The present day prices bear little resemblance to this early tariff either. The buildings round the harbour, which once served the needs of commercial craft, now cater for the growing tourist trade. One of those buildings was once a very profitable wee Post Office and it is said of a pufferman who married the postmistress that he didn't, that he actually married the profitable wee Post Office, but he never went back to sea and they lived happily ever after beside the Crinan Canal. You see, some books do have a happy ending!

BIBLIOGRAPHY

Jean Lindsay	The Canals of Scotland: David and Charles, 1968.
E.A.Pratt	Scottish Canals and Waterways: Selwyn and Blount, 1922.
A.D.Cameron	Getting to know... The Crinan Canal: the author, 1978.
Lesley MacDougall	The Crinan Canal: Famedram Publishers Ltd.
Dan McDonald	The Clyde Puffer: David and Charles, 1976.
George W. Burrows	Puffer Ahoy!: Brown, Son and Ferguson Ltd. 1981.
A.I.Bowman	Kirkintilloch Shipbuilding: Strathkelvin District Libraries and Museums, 1983.
Forsyth Hamilton	Kipper House Tales: The Michael Press, 1986.
Duckworth and Langmuir	West Highland Steamers: T. Stephenson and Sons Ltd. 1967.

ACKNOWLEDGEMENTS

I first travelled along the Crinan Canal on a glorious sunny autumn day, when the colours of the trees were at their height. It was an unforgettable experience and I hope I have managed to convey some of the magic I felt then and on subsequent visits to this beautiful wee canal.

I am indebted to Alec Howie of British Waterways for help with the drawing on page 20 and for his invaluable assistance and local knowledge. I am grateful too to Murdo MacDonald, archivist for Argyll and Bute District Council, whose local knowledge was also of great value and to the Forestry Commission for their specialist knowledge and information. Thanks too to George Waugh for his assistance in copying some of the photographs for publication and for the use of pictures on pages 14, 24 and 25. The marvellous song on page 35 was composed by Alex Mackenzie, who played Captain MacTaggart in the Maggie, for John Grieve, who played the engineer MacPhail in some of those BBC productions of The Vital Spark. John sang it in another puffer film called Highland Voyage and I am grateful to Douglas Gray, who made that film, for permission to use the words of the song. And talking of films, thanks too to Lumiere Pictures for permission to use the photograph on page 44. Thanks are also due to Tommy Lawton for help in finding some of this material.